THE MONSTER BOOK OF MONSTER TRUCKS

Quarto is the authority on a wide range of topics.
Quarto educates, entertains and enriches the lives of
our readers—enthusiasts and lovers of hands-on living.
www.quartoknows.com

Words in bold
are explained in
the glossary on
page 60

Author: Chris Oxlade
Editors: Cloud King Creative and Victoria Garrard
Designers: Cloud King Creative and Mike Henson
Picture Researcher: Sarah Bell

First published in 2020 by QEB Publishing,
an imprint of The Quarto Group.
26391 Crown Valley Parkway, Suite 220
Mission Viejo, CA 92691, USA
T +1 949 380 7510
F +1 949 380 7575
www.QuartoKnows.com

FSC
www.fsc.org

MIX
Paper from
responsible sources
FSC® C016973

A CIP record for this book is available from the Library of Congress.

ISBN 978-0-7112-5891-4

Printed in Singapore COS052020

9 8 7 6 5 4 3 2 1

CONTENTS

WHAT ARE MONSTER TRUCKS?

A monster truck is a **souped-up** pick up truck with massive wheels. It's built for jumping, racing, crushing old cars, and doing cool tricks.

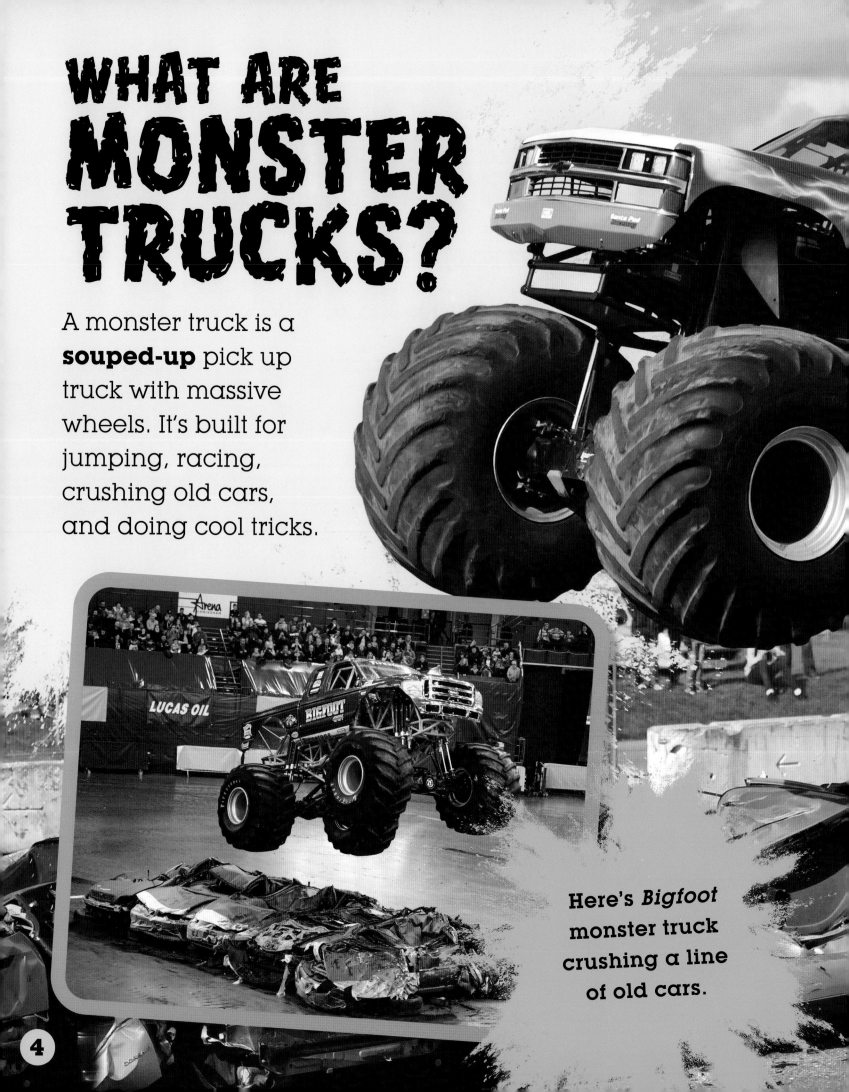

Here's *Bigfoot* monster truck crushing a line of old cars.

Here's *Grim Reaper* leaping over old cars to entertain the crowds.

Monster trucks have funny names such as *Grim Reaper*, *Swamp Thing*, and *Slingshot*.

GIANT WHEELS

Wow! Look at the size of those wheels! Giant wheels are what turn an ordinary truck into a monster truck. The massive chunky tires fit onto wide metal wheel rims.

Wheel rims

5.5 feet

Official monster truck racing tires are 5.5 feet tall and 3.7 feet wide.

All monster trucks are **4x4s**, which means the engine can supply power to all four wheels at the same time. Strong **brakes** on each wheel bring the truck to a quick stop.

Monster truck builders once used old tractor tires, but today tires are specially made for the trucks.

THE BIGGEST WHEELS

Giant wheels are not giant enough for some monster truck drivers! In 1986, Bob Chandler, who built the *Bigfoot* monster trucks, put gigantic wheels on *Bigfoot 5*.

Bigfoot 5 measures 15.5 feet tall. It weighs 18.7 tons and is the world's tallest monster truck.

Bigfoot 5's tires came from a US Army truck designed to drive through icy Alaska.

Each of *Bigfoot 5*'s wheels are 10 feet tall—so tall that you can stand inside them!

Can you spot the person standing underneath *Bigfoot 5*?

BOUNCY SUSPENSION

When a monster truck comes back to earth after a big jump, its wheels squash upward into the frame to soften the blow. The wheels are mounted on springy **suspension** that lets them move up and then pushes them down again.

Most monster truck's suspensions are made with **gas struts**. They are a bit like giant bicycle pumps.

Suspension makes the bumpy ride more comfortable for the driver.

Gas struts let the wheels move upward as much as 27.5 inches when the truck lands.

A STRONG FRAME

Monster trucks are heavy machines. They are always getting thrown around and bumped, so need to be very tough. Under a monster truck's body is a strong steel frame made of lots of tubes stuck together.

A monster truck's engine is 10 times as powerful as the engine in a family car.

A truck's frame is like a **skeleton**. It supports the truck's engine and other heavy parts.

MONSTER TRUCKING BEGINS

The history of monster trucking started in 1975, when an American construction worker named Bob Chandler started a business selling spare parts for pick up trucks in St. Louis.

Chandler had his own pick up truck that he drove for fun. He added giant wheels and a powerful engine to the truck. The first monster truck was born!

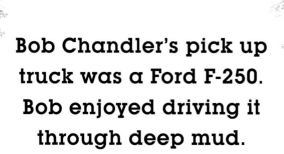

Bob Chandler's pick up truck was a Ford F-250. Bob enjoyed driving it through deep mud.

Bob Chandler's pick up truck on a **hill climb** challenge.

BIGFOOT SHOWS OFF

Jim Kramer was a friend of Bob Chandler, the man who built the first monster truck. It was Kramer who nicknamed Chandler's truck *Bigfoot*. In 1981 Bob tried crushing some old cars with *Bigfoot*. He was soon invited to car events to show off *Bigfoot*. Chandler then built a second truck, also called *Bigfoot*.

Bigfoot has no problem driving over cars with its huge wheels.

Here's the original *Bigfoot* performing at a monster truck show. It's one of the most famous monster trucks.

There are now more than 20 different *Bigfoot* monster trucks! This is number 17.

MORE MONSTER TRUCKS

Bigfoot was not the only monster truck on the scene. At the same time, another American, Jeff Dane, was building his own monster truck, called *King Kong*. The truck was named after the giant gorilla in the movie *King Kong*.

King Kong was a Ford pick up truck that had parts added from a 5.5-ton army truck.

Jeff Dane's *King Kong* first appeared in public in 1983. It raced against *Bigfoot* and other trucks including *Equalizer*.

18

The first *Equalizer* monster truck was built by Gary Cook and David Morris in 1988. This is what *Equalizer* looked like in 2003.

PAINTWORK

Monster truck owners like to design fantastic paintwork for their trucks. The trucks are painted as animals, aliens, monsters, and beasts, and given clever names. These detailed patterns and colors often take many hours to complete.

Monster truck *Spike* has paintwork that makes it look like a snarling dog.

Smashosaurus features beautiful yellow and orange scales and scary teeth!

Here's the *Monster Medic* monster truck. On the side is a one-eyed alien doctor!

21

BODY SHAPES

As well as having funny names and fantastic paint jobs, some monster trucks have wacky shapes too! Their bodies are shaped to look like wild animals, scary monsters, or aliens. The body is made from a material called **glass-reinforced plastic** (GRP for short) that can be **molded** into almost any shape.

Here's *Crushstation* doing a **wheelie** with its amazing lobster-shaped body.

This is *Jurassic Attack*, with its dinosaur's head, complete with horns.

The shape of *Brutus* makes the monster truck look like a dog with wheels!

23

MONSTER BEASTS

There are monster truck crocodiles, alligators, wolves, and even lobsters, each with its own funny name. The trucks are painted and shaped to resemble their animals.

Swamp Thing is designed as an alligator from a steamy swamp, complete with rows of sharp teeth.

Snake Bite looks
like it has two
white fangs on
its front grill!

25

MONSTER TRUCK RACING

Monster trucks race each other around circuits, tackling **obstacles** such as **earth ramps** and piles of old cars, and turning sharp corners. The drivers go as fast as they dare, fighting with the trucks to stop them from toppling over.

Samson zooms ahead of *Fullboar* in a race to the finish line.

The rear wheels turn as well as the front wheels, so the monster truck can take tight turns.

Rammunition monster truck takes a jump during an arena race.

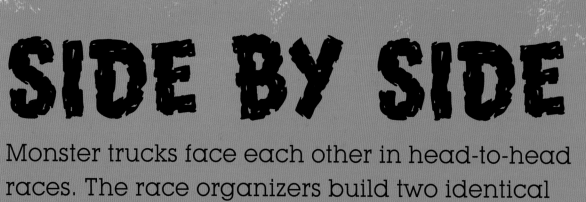

SIDE BY SIDE

Monster trucks face each other in head-to-head races. The race organizers build two identical courses, side by side. The trucks start at the same time and the first truck across the finish line wins the prize.

Raminator is just ahead of *Rammunition* as both trucks leap through the air.

Two monster trucks race each other over crushed-car obstacles.

TAKE OFF!

Jumping is a favorite trick for monster truck drivers. A driver **revs** up a truck's engine to get plenty of speed on the take-off ramp. But the truck mustn't go too fast, or too slow, or else the truck might **flip** backward or land with a crash.

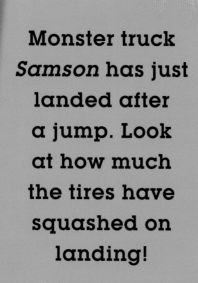

Monster truck *Samson* has just landed after a jump. Look at how much the tires have squashed on landing!

Here's *Bigfoot* 21, built in 2015, flying through the air with its wheels dangling underneath.

Bad Habit, its flag fluttering, flies high above the arena floor.

A RECORD LEAP

How far can a monster truck jump? A very long way. The monster truck *Bad Habit*, driven by owner Joe Sylvester, holds the world record. In 2013, *Bad Habit* made a colossal jump of 237 feet, 6 inches—that's three quarters the length of a soccer field!

Here's *Bad Habit* smashing in to some old cars after a massive jump.

Here's *Bad Habit* making its world-record leap over a super-long road truck.

Bad Habit took off from an earth ramp at 85 miles per hour and landed almost as fast!

FREESTYLE

Monster truck drivers love to show off tricks. This is called monster truck **freestyling**. On the list of tricks are jumps, tight turns, spins, **donuts**, wheelies, and flips. Freestyle competitions are part of monster truck shows.

Ghost Ryder monster truck doing a back flip.

Check out the *Big Pete* monster truck freestyling over flames and smashing through old campers!

WHEELIES AND FLIPS

To perform a wheelie, the monster truck driver revs up the engine and accelerates hard, making the front of the truck lift sharply. A flip is the most spectacular and most dangerous of all freestyle tricks. The truck hurtles at a steep wall, making the front of the truck flip up and over.

Monster truck *Samson* pulls off a wheelie while crushing cars.

Monster trucks like *Equalizer* have done back flips, front flips, and even double back flips!

Podzilla doing a wheelie. It's a skillful balancing act for the driver!

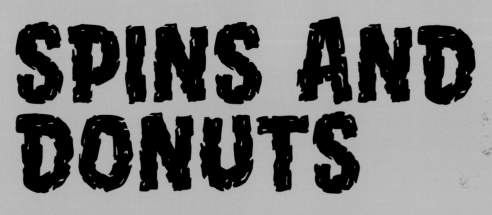

SPINS AND DONUTS

Monster trucks have all-wheel steering so they can spin around to make fast racing turns. Tight turns can turn into donuts—with high revs and the wheels turned hard to one side, the truck goes around and around in a dizzying spin, leaving a donut-shaped skid on the ground.

The spinning wheels throw up lots of dust as a monster truck hurtles around its donuts.

Spins and donuts
sometimes go wrong!

CAR CRUSHING

Crushing cars is the oldest form of monster trucking fun. It started way back in the 1980s with *Bigfoot*. Today **car-crushing** is a part of every monster truck event. A truck's mammoth wheels squash and scrunch the cars until they are almost flat.

This is the original *Bigfoot* truck fitted with double wheels for extra car-crushing fun!

Here's *Podzilla* rolling over a heap of old cars. *Podzilla* will roll backward and forward until the cars are wrecked.

MUD BOGGING

Some monster truck drivers enjoy the crazy sport of **mud bogging**. They drive their trucks into hollows filled with thick, deep mud to see if their trucks can struggle out of the sticky situations. They even try to tow other trucks out of the mucky goo!

Monster trucks need a good clean after a session of mud bogging!

Mud bogging is mucky! A truck's spinning wheel throw mud high in the air.

43

CRASH!

With monster trucks doing all those jumps, spin, wheelies, flips, and donuts, and hurtling around at high speed, accidents sometimes happen. The trucks can topple over sideways, flip over backward, or roll over and over with their wheels in the air.

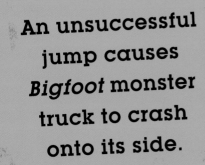

An unsuccessful jump causes *Bigfoot* monster truck to crash onto its side.

A monster truck lands with a terrible metal-grinding smash if the driver messes up a jump! Luckily there were no injuries.

Whoops! This monster truck has flipped over while freestyling on the beach, but no one was hurt.

45

STAYING SAFE

A monster truck must keep its driver safe if it's unfortunate enough to crash. There is a super-strong **roll cage** over the cab that protects the driver from being squashed if the truck rolls over. The driver is also strapped firmly into his or her seat with a **multi-point seatbelt**.

A truck's wheels are attached with wires in case they come loose in an accident. This stops the wheels flying dangerously into the air.

The driver has a
safety cut-out button
in the cab that stops
the engine and also
a fire extinguisher.

DRIVING MONSTER TRUCKS

It takes hours and hours of practice to learn to control a powerful monster truck and to perform jumps, donuts, and other tricks. A monster truck's controls are just like a car—there's an accelerator to add power, strong brakes to slow the truck down, and powered steering.

The best drivers are as famous as their monster trucks, such as Josh "Vinny Venom" Gibson.

It takes a team of mechanics to service and repair a monster truck to keep the truck running.

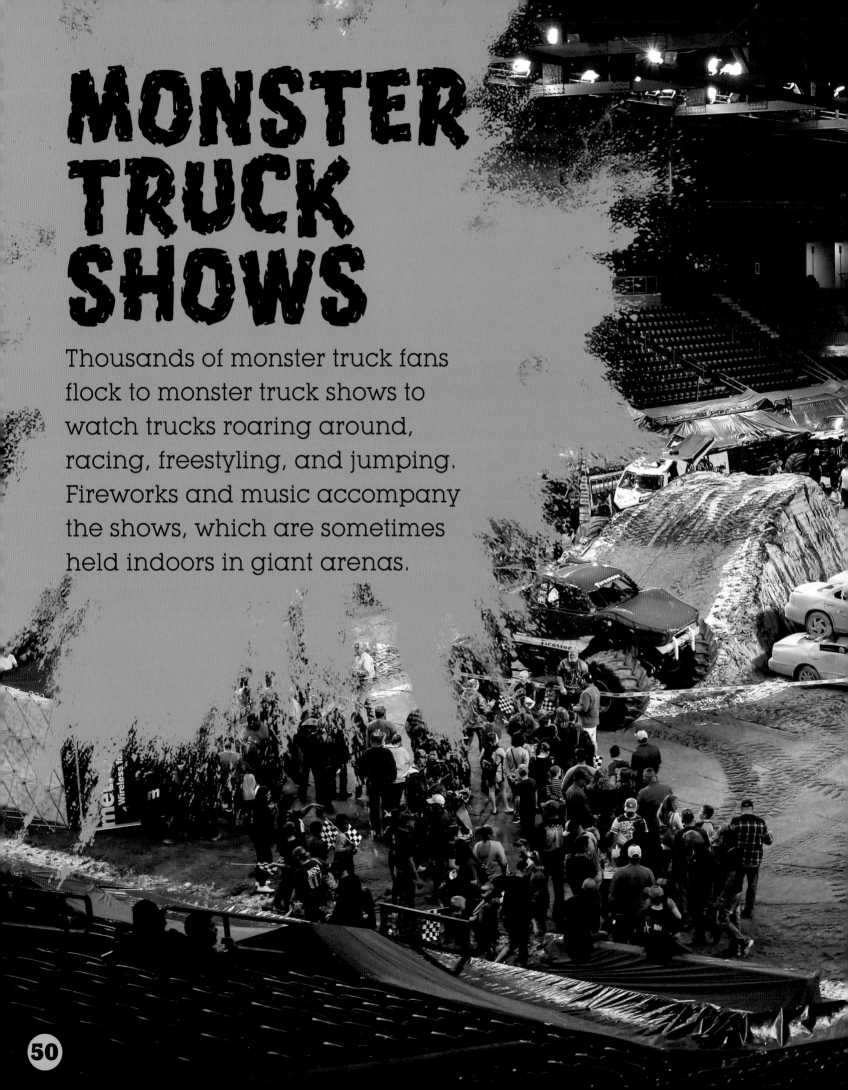

MONSTER TRUCK SHOWS

Thousands of monster truck fans flock to monster truck shows to watch trucks roaring around, racing, freestyling, and jumping. Fireworks and music accompany the shows, which are sometimes held indoors in giant arenas.

Fans have the chance to meet their heroes for photos and selfies.

Monster truck fans get a chance to look closely at the trucks, climb on board, and even take rides in the trucks.

51

MONSTER MONSTERS

All monster trucks are monster machines, but some monster trucks are bigger than others! *Big Pete* and *Axe* are two examples of these super-monster trucks. *Big Pete* is a monster truck built from the tractor unit of an **articulated** truck with giant wheels added.

The body of *Axe* monster truck is based on an American fire truck and is run by Team Scream.

Here's *Big Pete* entertaining a crowd by jumping over a line of old cars.

WACKY MONSTERS

Some monster truck drivers love to build out-of-the-ordinary monster trucks. These wacky machines really turn heads at monster truck shows! Party-goers enjoy setting out for the night in monster truck limousines like the 33-foot, 12-seater *Hustler*.

ACHINE

Higher Education is a monster school bus! In fact, it's a fairly normal monster truck with a bus-shaped body bolted on.

Monster truck limousines have a very long, very strong frame to support the body between the wheels.

MINI MONSTERS

Monster trucks are all about being big, so it seems strange that anyone would create a mini monster truck. But they do. These mini monsters are built for young monster truck racers who want to experience the thrills of driving before progressing to the real thing.

Miss Mini Patrol **has bright flashing lights for night-time arena shows.**

Here's a mini monster truck called *Miss Mini Patrol* taking a leap from an earth ramp.

RADIO CONTROL

Not all of us can build and drive a real-life monster truck! But we can all experience the fun of monster trucks with fantastic radio-control models. With plenty of practice, drivers can perfect monster truck maneuvers such as donuts and flips.

Radio-controlled (RC) monster trucks don't mind splashing through puddles.